Bro

Healing Words

A Collection of Poetry through Grief

Austie M. Baird
-Editor, Cover Artist-

Austie M. Baird is a born and raised Oregonian, holding both History and Education degrees from Eastern Oregon University. Long before becoming a wife and mother, Baird connected with the power of the written word, finding healing properties in both reading and writing. She draws strength from the beauty that surrounds her and the overwhelming love of her family.

A.B.Baird Publishing
Oregon, USA

Printed in the United States of America

First Printing, 2019

ISBN: 9781949321098

Cover Art Image by Austie M. Baird

A.B.Baird Publishing
66548 Highway 203
La Grande OR, 97850
USA

www.abbairdpublishing.com

Dear Readers,

As always, we at A.B.Baird Publishing believe that all our writers are incredibly talented and encourage you to explore new writers often! You can find the Instagram handles for the writers listed at the front of the book.

Our goals here at A.B.Baird Publishing center on continuing to empower writers by giving social media based authors as many avenues as possible towards publication. If you are interested in how you can become published, or want to stay up to date on our latest ventures, please join our email list on our website www.abbairdpublishing.com or visit us on instagram @a.b.baird_publishing.

Your reviews mean more to us than you realize! One of the keys to continued success is having reviews on sites such as Amazon. If you have enjoyed this anthology we as that you please let us know by leaving reviews on the amazon listing. In addition we always encourage you to check out the authors on their social media accounts and let them know what you think of their work!

Thank you for your support- without you, we would be nothing!

Austie Baird – Owner
A.B.Baird Publishing

Table of Contents

This anthology, born of grief and healing, is dedicated to all of the souls who have left us and to all of those of us who have been left behind. May each of you find comfort in your suffering, joy in your pain, and healing in your tears.

The Longest Goodbye

We sit
your hand in mine
for days, weeks, months
at a time
not a single word
between us
but the quiet beauty
of our Love
resonating like an
old familiar song
melodic in our bond

You don't know this place
can't place my face
but you know that I am Love
as you drift away
and that is enough for me
needs to be
enough for me
as your eyes grow wide
searching for safety
lost in long forgotten places
they fall on me
peacefully
your hand clings to mine
ceaselessly

I hold your fears steady
as our memories treasured
float like feathers
on a breeze
leaving behind
another missing piece
of our story
another page blurring
ink smearing
words disappearing
line by line

As we sit
your hand in mine
saying the longest goodbye

-Abi Hayes-

Warfare

I'm drowning in his veins. His heart, twice the size it should be, pumping tainted blood through the labyrinth buried beneath his skin. I take refuge in his lungs. And it's then that I see what's creating the cataract of sludge. Great piles of charred mess building across the walls. Too hot, poisoned air launched at me and him with kamikaze apathy and sniper-like precision. And all the while he spits the scorched oxygen to his heart. Cranking out more pollution than his body can dispose of. And me with my gas mask, hell-bent on tearing down the filth. I shovel it out like a chimney sweep in a stack that's still on fire. Until my energy is spent. Until the tears stream hot and sulfurous, only adding to the contaminated blood. And I hope that if I stay here, a living thing inside of him, that the air that falls in on me will somehow be clean. That I can breathe life back into him. But the sky above me is filled with explosions of darkness. And the bombs only continue to fall.

-Emily Perkovich-

Preserved

roses are bleeding and trees are weeping
as she exhaled her last breath
her body lain down in the valley of sorrow
where for eternity she would be sleeping
as snow covered her flesh
like a blanket of comfort
spring would cover her in flowers
like a memory preserved
as all endings have new beginnings
for there is life after death

-Lizzy in words-

Unknown

it was in the silence that I knew,
in the silence,
where I grew,
where I grew,
touching you,
watching you,
knowing, too,
that no silence could falter,
no quiet would alter,
what nature had driven,
toward love,
hearts had given,
in beats,
rising, falling,
sun heats,
setting, calling,
to worlds too enthralling,
two worlds,
silent,
stalling,

sun, rise,
silent morning,
sun, rise,
silence, mourning,
through eyes,
sleep had flown,
two eyes knew,

unknown.

-J. Savarese-

Returning to Silt

You say you feel sadness
when you see a flower wilting,
it's leaves curling
and chlorophyll drying.

You feel sadness in seeing
his petals turning brown and
becoming sunken and
dehydrated
even though it had
rained
just the day
before.

You watch him digress,
losing basic independences,
dropping petals
one
by
one.

You feel sadness as
he nears the end
of life. But-

there is beauty
as we watch all
the silken petals fall:
nature invites nostalgia
to watch their descents and
review all the moments
which explain what
he had achieved
And what we will
miss.

His petals will wither and
his leaves will become crisp
like in autumn, and
we will feel sadness,
but-
this moment of natural deterioration
of petals parting
from stem and
returning to silt,
will be eternally etched
into our memories.

We are fathered
to witness him.
we are gathered to recall
why he lived and
why he let go.

There is nothing more beautiful
than the tuning of the orchestra
before their powerful finale.
nothing more peaceful
than the last page being read
And a book being returned
To its shelf.

-Jamie Rhiannon Fehribach-

Breathing

life is simply a breath in the body of death

-Brianne Reilly-

Out of Time

there where the hourglass runs out
and the clock no longer ticks
there my sweet child I'll be waiting
where time no longer exists

-Lizzy in words-

Diamante

Life
Paths, Journey
Experiencing, Growing, Failing
Goals, Morals, Memories, Time
Aging, Reminiscing, Leaving
End, Crossroads
Death

-Aliya Ameer-

Throes

I don't know what it is, but it's black, and it's filling him up. And if I could I would pull it from his body. If I could I would eat it as my last meal. And I fly to him just to try. I hold his hand and hope that my pressure and my voice can drown the darkness. I hope I can pull the damned thing from him and swallow it myself. Snuff me out but please don't take him. I supplicate as though I could coerce my light to fill him and banish what has taken him over. His words come as lilting breaths. Something just short of a whisper, yet still carrying his cadence. And he wants to leave. But I cannot let him. And I hold onto him, though he assures me I must let go. I must let go, though I crave to carry his contagion. His contagion, my very own albatross. And as the shadows overwhelm him, ragged and shallow breaths struggle to sustain him. But it is only a murky twilight leading into the complete void of midnight. And I don't know the last time my eyes were dry, but I know it was dark just before. I know I held his hand, and the blackened disease circled our wrists. And that darkness never left him. It consumed me, but it somehow never left him. And I don't know how, but it took him instead of me. And here I am. And everything is black.

-Emily Perkovich-

Final

I will take it from here
as your cheek is brushed
by your last tear
time to let go
one final breath
I will take it from here
as you lay down to rest
I will carry your heart
out into the world
so you are not lost
your love, always near
beyond death do us part
I carry you in here

-Lizzy in words-

Gladioli

lost
your battle
still my champion
gladiolus on your tomb
forever

-Bianca van der Kamp-

My Sister's Grief

searing shock
cleaves open their heart
contorting her body
tearing apart

saltwater streaming
drenching her face
clutching for siblings
to tightly embrace

her wailing so deep
a piercing refrain
bursts open their grief
till a stillness remains

reality strikes
a withering hue
agony emerges
to torment anew

the youngest, her son
emerged from her flesh
from infant to manhood
lives closely enmeshed

killed by another
in a frenzied attack
murderous violence
there's no turning back

taken in seconds
a son and a brother
a nephew, a friend
a mate and a lover

sorrow so deep
drowning her soul
a lifetime of bonds
she'll never feel whole

at peace, laid to rest
home soil he lies under
this place grew the man
tore his family asunder

-Kathy Coutts-

Heaven is Beside You Now

Heaven is beside you now as you look upon the banner of life
The loss of humanity flashes truth in livid sky
As your tears nourish the earth with noble truth and wisdom
Stolen moments of life gaze bewildered at memories collected in sacred springs
Reflections of exuberant spirit sparkle in streams of sovereignty
Murmurs of a language transcendent in nature
immerse you in exquisite tones
Echoes of earth fade as angel's sing tunes of enlightenment
Find peace now, as your anguished heart mourns the loss of time
Rest easy now, among the candescent shimmers of light, as they comfort you in your sadness
Clouds of silver and gold hold you in radiant light looking past eternal grave
Shades protect you from the blazing heat of suffering, as you embrace cascading droplets of
hope and peace
Engulfed in luminosity, iridescent liquid floods into the essence of those you love
You are blessed within our hearts as you engage your spirit in holy bliss
A vestige of love once held will forever shine as treasures in divine sky
Rays of hope cherish your soul for eternity
As flowers bloom to the abundance of everlasting love, you are forever in our hearts

-Sinead McGuigan-

Tears

they say that tears are prayers
that you cannot say out loud
so I hope that God can see
how much I'm crying every night

-Lizzy in words-

Again

There will be tears again,
but they will be different.
They will be the kind
you can't stem the flow of
with phrases like,
'Things will change' or
'Everything will turn out ok.'
Because what happened is
the most solid piece of stone
that has blocked my path
in the timeline of my life.
No matter how
I rework the events,
this cannot change.
Will not change.

Words will not mend it.

-Jamie Rhiannon Fehribach-

Numbers

How does one measure a relationship?
Is it in the infinite number of calls or texts?
How often you see each other, or how frequent you bed?

For me it's not something to be measured quantitatively.
It's all about the substance of your relationship – a qualitative measurement.

Every moment we spent together ignited my soul.
He always made sure our senses were fully engaged,
indulging not only in each other's company,
but all the magical experiences life happened to present us...

169 The number of days in my reverie with him

7 The number of full moons we shared

37 The number of minutes he held my hand on our way home, while I drove, and he slept (the last night I saw him)

01-06; The exact moment the floor fell out, and my heart shattered…

08:03 when I got the call that his had stopped.

-Whiskey + Empathy-

Unshed, Unseen

We stand silent
Dancing in drops of regret
That fall from this tear stained sky.

Greys streak blues
As eyes blink back emotions aborted
Denied the space and time
To form into full-fledged life.

Winds shifting skirts around pale legs
As hopes are lowered
One last time
Into the cradling arms
Of this cold ground.

-Austie M. Baird-

Gone

We were
And we had
And now
We won't

-Greg Oman-

Slipping From My Hands

I see the twinkling of the stars,
but I do not hear them sing.

I see the rustling of the leaves,
but I do not feel the wind.

I see the parting of the clouds,
but I do not dare enter in.

I hold a smooth stone in my hands,
but I only feel the pain.

I hold a dream close to my heart,
but I only see it fading.

I hold the memories of yesterday,
but I slowly let them go
slipping from my hands.

-Mark Wayne-

Snow

my heart makes the sound
of fresh snow under your feet
forever changed
until time covers it under a fresh layer
though never quite the same
it sits there still and buried deep
all cracked and bruised
like snow beneath your feet

-Lizzy in words-

Light as a Feather

"Light as a feather, stiff as a board; Light as a feather, stiff as a board…"

Rigor mor'tis sets in,
and the weight of you sinks,
like a stone,
settling in the pit of my stomach.

The ripples reverberate,
from my core out through my body.

Unable to breathe, I gasp for air.
Instead, the formaldehyde I inhale spasms my lungs, and stings my eyes...

Tears fall.

How I wish to be weightless;
To feel that happiness again;
The way your presence lifted my soul.
sigh

"Light as a feather, stiff as a board; Light as a feather, stiff as a board…"

-Whiskey + Empathy-

Darkness

My eyes open to the beauty of the sun dawning but this darkness is so addictive that I tend to draw the curtains.

-Vivek-

Resting Next to Them

Thoughtful memorial, I was tender, more youthful
then.

Here and now, the action of arranging white blossoms
plunge through to a harvest of butterflies
gone sour.
I no longer have the breadth to store or suppress.

Stood and I stare at their cemetery stones,
catching cold, coming to grips with
beliefs
I will never know how to define.

With little left to claim, such pioneers are we
to barely exist.

I have set teeth against head stone, my mouth bare
to borrowed ground.

I want to organize my bones and bury beneath.

In the mute secrecy that is death,
I long for rest
next to them.

-Steve Zmijewski-

Balancing Acts of Grief

Grief deposits you
On tippy top peaks,
Mountain precipices.
Balanced precariously,
Between invisible forces;

As you fight battles without warriors:
Self-stitching lacerations without blood.

Consumed with finding balance
To keep from falling
This way
-Or that-
There is no time
-No desire-
To examine the world around.

Unhearing what you see,
Unseeing what you hear,
Never feeling able to bring yourself,
To give more than casual care
Least the weight of your attentions

Tip the scales
And leave Jack
Chasing Jill

Tumbling
Tumbling
Down some forlorn hill.

-Austie M. Baird-

When You Left

When you left
I don't suppose you did see
what you would leave me

You left me endless search
of a sense of self
where do I belong, which is my day?

You left me hundred questions
wrapped in guilt and shame
what did I do, to send you away?

You left me a silence
unarticulated grief
how do I speak now, what do I say?

You left me a legacy
of loving and loss
of constantly leaving, I don't know how to stay

When you left
I don't suppose you did see
the loss it would mean for me

When you left

-Rachna-

What Am I Feeling?

What am I feeling?
What is this called?
I have no excitement for the future that I got.
I used to hate being patient but now I'm waiting for so long.
No expectations from life, no happy thoughts.
Always waiting for the worst, for the challenges to be brought.
I'm standing still inside the battlefield, in the war.
Life will take whatever it want's, steals my precious treasures takes
them to God.
They say It's not your fault it happens to us all.
Tell them to stop the same old stories, sympathy and sad thoughts,
it doesn't help, it's not what I want.
life made a special place for my precious inside my heart.
It let's me pretend I'm protecting them at all cost
then takes them away to the unknown, to the farthest, to the far.
Pulls their place from the roots of my heart, leaves forever the painful
scars.

-Samman-

Shadows

sometimes I see a flickering
of the beauty that life holds
but the shadows that I carry
how do I get rid of those

-Lizzy in words-

Lost, After the Storm

The storm hit without a warning and ripped away her anchor. One after the other, waves crashed down upon her. Gasping for air, it took all she had to keep herself from drowning.

Eventually things began to settle, but her world had been violently shaken and turned upside down. Without an anchor, she wound up in the middle of nowhere drifting aimlessly at sea – lost.

Completely disheveled and emotionally exhausted, she lie on the remains of her vessel, heartbroken, and thought back on all the signs she ignored... the heavy pit in her stomach, the ring around the moon, and that dream... that damn dream she couldn't shake –

> *They were enjoying the beautiful Spring day walking around Storm King when she heard a voice whisper in her ear, "Time is almost up." Startled, she turned to see a strange figure pointing away. Following its direction, she realized they were now in a cemetery. He was sitting near a grave alone, drinking. Along came a crow, and as it softly landed on the headstone, she finally woke up.*

Now she would give anything to wake up from this nightmare. But the pain searing in her lungs and hot sun beating down proved this was her reality...
She was lost; He was lost, forever; Everything she owned, everything they shared
– lost.

And then something glimmering in the sun's reflection caught her eye. She slowly reached out, her fingers searching, then grasping the small familiar object – but how could it be? In her hands she held the pendant He had made for her from the single pearl he found months back. She had lost this in the storm along with everything else, yet somehow it found her again. And as the tears rolled down her cheeks, back into the sea, she felt the tiniest sliver of hope – all because of that precious pearl that had no value, but to her, was profoundly priceless...

-Whiskey + Empathy-

A Beautiful Dance

It was a beautiful song,
that unexpectedly came along.

A knife pierced his heart,
is the end where it all starts.
The ache inside lingers still,
death is life's toughest pill.

He willingly drank the warm nectar,
as demons laughed at the specter.
She laid so still and ashen white,
no breath and eyes void of sight.

Evil giggles and celebrates,
thinking it has won this round of fate.
He stares in silent misery,
wondering if he, she is able to see.

The razor fangs of fate sunk deep,
taking what he held but could not keep.
Remains the memories of days,
two tortured souls, and one could not stay.

It was a beautiful dance,
that all happened by chance.

-Mark Wayne-

Rock Bottom

The rock bottom which I stepped on each day,
Drowns me in to the deep ocean,
Suffocating and unconscious under my skin,
Where, the purpose of life showcases a glimpse of joy and sadness.

There was no help given,
To avoid, sinking in the ocean.
And it reminded me that I still can't swim,
The waves grabbed me and covered like a bubble.

Drowning to the minute of the death,
I saw flashes of the life I lived,
And recognised I didn't built any immortal castles,
I clutched myself and tried hard to come back to life.
And I was told, there will be silent nights for the rest of my life.
For once gone,
Will never come back.

-Akshaya Premnath A.-

Extinguished

There is a heaviness.
That sits in the soul.

All I can think,
Is that it must be mirroring
The dark that now exists
Where your smile
Used to be.

-Austie M. Baird-

A Future Stolen

The difficult part was not in letting you go –
There was nothing wrong, or damaging, with keeping you in my heart.

It was the vision I had of "us" that felt toxic.
It was the idea of a future we would never have that killed me,
over and over.

All the imagined possibilities dissipated the day you were taken.

So why then, did they seem more vivid than ever… now; after?

-Whiskey + Empathy-

So It Ends

You could see them from miles away, right in the middle of an unending carpet of dandelions, shaded by cotton candy clouds.

He was an Aghori, tugging away at the singed corpse of their relationship, while she stood next to him, all pristine, pointing at the sweet-meats.

As they marveled at the delicious fragments of the corpse, they were once again whole; enjoying a tender moment as they devoured the succulent offering of the past.

Once full, they walked away in opposite directions; Their feet crushing the delicate dandelions, blaming each other for having eaten the most "delightful" parts.

-Alick Bailey-

Muse

The pounding in my chest
That I feel upon waking each morning recently
Reminds me of how it felt
To be ever so close
To the one
That has been keeping me
At the edge
Of my seat
Feeding
The flames within me
That are still burning
Afraid to fade
In to the darkness
Where I may or may not see
That this pounding in my chest
Is that of a heart
Slowly breaking
At the feet
Of the one
I call
    My muse

-Courtney Blackstone-

Sometimes

left clutching the
banister
sometimes
patience is a virtue

light
as a feather
or stiff
as a board
sometimes
death is a gift

and the instant it steals
when the arrow
storms through

I'll be seeing you
again
and soon
I'll be seeing you

-Steve Zmijewski-

The Sun Will Rise

Tomorrow morning the sun will rise
Life will be seen through tear stained eyes
In hope I'll search for you in the changing skies
Admitting you are gone is the cruelest of lies.

-Nikki C. Mercer-

Another Day to Your Name

Another day with your name,
Like the Ayaat to protect myself
From the world that is filled
With filth and sins.

Another day to your name
For the lips forgot how it is
To pray and now it prays only
With a single word that makes
Worth everything to live for.

Another day with your name
For the nights are turning dark and
You are the only source of light
Through this labyrinthine maze -
My life.

Another day to your name
For in the lost times, you are
The anchor that holds me
To the ground, telling me
Where I stand in our lives.

Another day with your name for
You made me learn the meaning
Of how to feel beyond my control,
And feel with everything and
More.

Another day to your name
For this oblivion prolonged
And now there is only one hope -
You, in the lonely and crowded world.

Another day and all days
To your name.

-Samira Rahman-

Fade to Black – Revisited

Slowly you drifted away and could not stay
You are not coming back so gently fade to black

Vacant staring eyes I watched your demise
You took all I knew and you took my future too
You took all my dreams and you took nothing it seems

I cannot be who they want me to be
For they always want too much of me

Staring into the unknown and alone into the alone
Everything has gone dark and my barely beating heart
Distant bells faintly toll as heaven claimed another soul

I pray for a light to chase the endless night
The love and mercy I lack before I fade to black

-Mark Wayne-

My Apple A Day

My apple a day seems to keep everyone away, so I'll take two aspirin and call myself in the morning. I'll write a prescription for all my lost loves. I'll lie down on the couch and ask myself, "how does this make you feel?" I'll try to convince myself that someone actually gives a damn.

-Stacy Evans B-

Exulansis

The more I tried to let it out, free myself, the more alone I felt.
Each attempt to share the burden I carried with me,
met with awkward silence or nervous dismissal.

So I would swallow it down further…
Chased with whatever the tonic of the day happened to be;
Attempting to erase the bitter aftertaste, like some bad childhood medicine.

And I learned to lie and fake it,
so when they asked me how I was doing,
my smile reassured them and put them at ease.

My pain lingering on the evening fog for only me to feel
when it would roll back in –

Wash it down, and smile once again.

-Whiskey+Empathy-

Pieces

There are not enough pieces of me
To fill the holes left by you

-Mark Wayne-

Goodbyes

I cry myself to sleep at night
afraid of what's to come
to walk into a house each day
that's no longer your home
to never feel your touch again
linger on my skin
no kiss hello or kiss goodbye
only tears and wondering why
why you had to be the one
that God needed so much
if only I could hold you close
and feel once more your touch

-Lizzy in words-

Gracious Hostess

Only the waterproof mascara will do for these days,
For I am walking gingerly
In the season of grief,
And these tears do not generally
Announce their coming,
Like good guests should do.

But I learned how to play hostess from you.

-Austie M. Baird-

Fallen

As I let the memories from that weekend a year ago wash over me, I tried to recall the moment I fell…

Was it the moment we stated in unison, "We'll have the shishito peppers," without discussing it prior, when the waiter asked us if we knew what we wanted?

Or when we heard a band playing Latin music while we were walking, and you pulled me inside to dance?

Perhaps it was the early morning walk along the boardwalk, where you opened up to me, and we talked for hours?

Or the time we spent before the wedding, and the way you looked at me, dressed up in your suspenders as I helped you with your bow tie?

Maybe it happened while I was wrapped in your arms as we leaned against the building, watching the McGregor / Mayweather match across the street in some stranger's apartment?

Or when you woke up in the middle of the night to comfort me, at a time when comfort seemed futile?

I can't recall the exact moment.
I guess it doesn't matter now, and maybe it never really did.
I just know that weekend was when I fell. And it scared the shit out of me.
I never told you all the times we were together after;
And now this is my only means…

-Whiskey + Empathy-

Temporary

Your temporary presence in my life
Left a permanent absence in my heart

-Nikki C. Mercer-

After Midnight

It is 12:02am and I find myself wondering
If grief stricken memories and the dreams
They bring are more real after midnight

-Mark Wayne-

Displacement

Two places
Two worlds
Connected dots
One mind severed
Tears and smiles
Both falling
And expanding
Neither here
Nor there
Torn and mending

-Greg Oman-

Unfulfilled Story

Alive or dead,
In between slipping –
Consciousness and unconsciousness.

The pleasure of a pain
Of the emotions I feel within and
The holding on to hopes that
I refuse to let fade;
Memories are just that – memories
Like a tale of a fairytale that
Morphed into my worst nightmares,
A sense of being forever a loner
And desolate life of loneliness.

Promises turned to ashes,
Thousands of vows turned to
Sweet nothingness;
Dust became those endless dusks
And dawns lost in each other's arms –
All gone.

Who said that love fulfills
Everything and comes true
For all?

-Samira Rahman-

Delicate Now

Delicate are the times
Of yester-year
When we did reap
What we sow
Where fondness strummed
A healing tune
Desperate are the times
Of the fleeting now
Pinned upon a ticking wall
Where hindsight claws
Its masterful rendition

-Greg Oman-

She Always Hated Her Eyes

She always hated her eyes,
She said they were so plain and dark
But she never knew that every time I looked into them
I got lost in the galaxies
That were reflected within them,
And my body was set on fire when I saw the flowing embers deep within her soul.

-Starr-

Emerald

one glance is all that it usually takes to sway me ever so eagerly in your direction
a pull from an emerald sea, it isn't long until I am drowning
yet I cannot fathom wanting to breathe again
if it means that I would have to leave you
to come up for air
I suppose this means
I would rather die
loving you
than to live
a single day
pretending that I don't

-Courtney Blackstone-

The Mermaid's Lament

Every now and then,
when the grief washed over her in an unbearable wave,
she'd replay the recordings.

Ripping her chest open,
reliving the memories and the feelings,
for just a moment,
just to hear his voice...

Her Sailor —
Torn away far too soon.

-Whiskey + Empathy-

Forgiveness

I've been trying to forgive myself
even though there is no blame
life just happened and then you died
but somehow I keep thinking
that I could have done more
maybe if I connected things sooner
or if I was more aware
maybe then I could have saved you
knowing that blaming myself isn't fair

-Lizzy in words-

The Power and Responsibility of Words

These broken hearts
are like exploding cannonballs
tick-tocking to a halt, caught in slow motion
across the horizontal layers of time,
carrying acres of pain over the years
inflicting ruin and starting arson flames
in other hearts that were once whole.

These broken hearts are heavy
abundant in reckless love, hidden in fear
but hungrily greedy for the gentle touch
of spring's breeze as they bear alone
the harsh winds of winter,
bracing themselves for endless cold,
buried to the top in ice and snow
waiting for the sun to thaw and warm
their dry and weary bones.

These broken hearts
need compassionate words to restore
their broken, darkened minds
in hearts that have become too fragile
from constant evil whispers in their soul
telling them they are too damaged
to ever return to have a different destiny.

These broken hearts search the world
for kind words to salve their wounds,
to break their chains from imprisonment,
to build anew their cities with life once more
and for someone to call their own.

These broken hearts need healing words
to remember that through their scars
they have transformed into a lighthouse
to save other shattered and defeated hearts
lying forgotten in storm-tossed wreckages.

These broken hearts need healing words
to redeem themselves for they are
and have always been
divinely worthy.

-Reena Doss-

Where is the Grace

Where is the grace when the moment is done?
Words I wanted to say
Hang heavy in the air
Too late for regrets
For all I can do is
Silently scream
Where is the grace as I begin to come undone?
Where is the grace as the lonely moments slowly pass?
Where is the grace when the dark night forever lasts?
Where is the grace when the ghosts are all too real?
Where is the grace when the silence is all I feel?
Where is the grace when the final bell tolls?
When the pain inside
Is all too real
Too late for regrets
For the end is here
And my fate is sealed
Where is the grace in exchange for my soul?

-Mark Wayne-

Scarred

there's a crater of salt carved in my skin
where a river of tears flows down to my chin
a landscape
through worries and stress defined
one that's no exception to wrinkles and lines

-Lizzy in words-

But Grief Remains

Spring sprang to summer
Summer rushed to fall
Skipping beauty in falling leaves
Winters chill withers all.

All has changed
Nothing the same
Landscapes moving, unimpeded dream.

But the grief,
The grief
Remains.

-Austie M. Baird-

Empty Air

Laying in the dark
Crushed
By the silence
Of empty air
Where your breathing
Used to
Gently lull
Me to sleep

-Mark Wayne-

Slumber

a quake
sleeps in the trenches
of my chest
the sadness
tip toes silently
through my veins
a failed attempt
to starve
the whispers
of my longing
that have become
the alarm
that awakens
the quake
my heart
in ruins
my hands
wander
my soul
wonders
if it will rest best
in the soil
where your bones
now slumber

-Courtney Blackstone-

What Will Remain

I. these blinds that never close quite right. the whisper of golden morning light through their crooked teeth. the amber warmth on my skin.

II. the creak of these floorboards. these bones.

III. stargazer lilies.

IV. the summer rain smile of the old scottish man behind the pharmacy counter. his puddled eyes when he tells me of glasgow.

V. chocolate. all of it.

VI. two sets of small hands willing to hold my heartbeat any time it gets too heavy.

VII. campfires. their soothing smoke and crackling laughter. their arms waving light to the sky.

VIII. the hole worn in the hem of my softest tee shirt. your scent on the collar. sandalwood, cedar, and sunsets.

IX. the towering oak in the backyard. its blanketing shade. its grandmotherly voice singing the breeze through my hair.

X. your memory.

XI. the hurt. forever, maybe. and that's okay.

XII. hope. that sweet, feathered thing.

XIII. myself.
XIV. myself.
XV. myself.

-Emily May Portillo-

Undone

could you wrap your arms around me
so I can come undone
could you hold onto me tightly
as all that's left is to succumb
while I shatter into pieces
and I fall to the floor
could you keep them all together
I have the strength no more
could you wrap your arms around me
so I can catch my breath
just for a little while
until the sadness has left

-Lizzy in words-

Silhouettes

Memories over time
Fade until…
Nothing is left
But the silhouettes

-Mark Wayne-

Next to Me

I breathe it in
this place called home
the scent of summer grass
freshly mown
I hear the familiar melodies
of songbirds stirring
forgotten memories

now the lyrics linger
hauntingly
my heart sings
a little off-key;
it's not the place
it used to be

when you were here

Next to me

-Abi Hayes-

Celebratory Checklists

Celebrating the things that are
Is simply a reminder
Of those
That are
Not.

-Austie M. Baird-

Wish You Were Here

how i wish you were here to see
what a lovely man i have met
how i wish you were here to be
at the wedding we've not had yet

how i wish you were here to watch
my daughters' musical debut
how i wish you were here to be
the token audience yahoo

how i wish you were here to laugh
at my grandpa inspired jokes
how i wish you were here to view
the many eye rolls they invoke

how i wish you were here to feel
the sadness your absence does make
how i wish you were here to heal
my mother's terrible heartache

how i wish you were here to sing
happy birthday to those you love
how i wish you were here with us
instead of watching from above

while i wish you were here to play
the drums to your favorite song
you have been here in our hearts
where your memory does live on

-Krystal Centinello-

Frame

What to give-
And what to let go
To watch you walk
Through that door
A grin, to all smiles
Lightened hearts
Brightly lit
And forgive my fading memory
It has been forever

-Greg Oman-

In-between

that moment between wake and sleep
where your mind is fully open
where you can see things far beyond the borders of this world
a state of enlightenment, some would say
where your mind can see into another realm
that is where we meet
where I can feel your breath upon my skin
your arms holding me

-Lizzy in words-

Heart Strings and Other Broken Things.

It's heart strings and other broken things,
Crushed veneers, trust and promises
And the heart's recall of being whole,
It's sleepless nights and love you cannot mend,
Like the young boy you were seeing a car crash for the first time
And wondering how metal could bend.

It's wondering whether you could steal back the words
Make them secret,
Un-see their lips form a storm that breaks against you,
Their mouth forming silent words that ring out as a swell,
I'm leaving.
And in the silence of her eyes you understand
Why sailors used to tie themselves to the mast.

It's lying awake and begging not to dream,
It's wishing to forget but being unable to abandon
Memories of someone who was with you even as you slept,
The bed seems as broken as the body within
Without the one you shared it with,
And waking alone you regret another day has come.

It's pain and nothing else.
It's loving someone and knowing it's not enough,
It's thinking of them every time your heart declines to beat
It's bearing whilst wishing you could fight the quiet.
To hear their voice and make them laugh
Put all the broken pieces back,
And beg them for a second chance.

It's trying to heal and knowing
Some wounds will last for life,
It's leaving bruises on your knees
Clasping hands until they bleed,

Praying for them to come back,
Putting miracles in motion
In a world that doesn't believe,
But hope is all you have
And that might not be enough,
But it's all you have,
Without the one you love.

-Greg Rowan Shearer-

Firsts

they're all for you
every breath I take
because all those firsts without you
they ache

-Lizzy in words-

Your Image

Memories remain
And you never
Change
Your image
Frozen in time
Is forever etched
In my troubled mind

-Mark Wayne-

Lucy

I look up to the stars
searching for answers.
The only person I'm looking for
is you.
Can you see me?
Or am I just watching the clouds
float on by.
Life has become a living nightmare.
I know that you would have all the answers.
But I've forgotten the sound of your voice
it has been so long.
I think about you all the time
wishing you were here.
I can't change our past,
but I can change my future.
Sadly life goes on without you
but I still cling to our memories
hoping that one day
I will see you again.

-Amy Littleford-

Wandered

you are wilderness
I have wandered
with feet from
a previous life

-Courtney Blackstone-

Grieving

don't tell me that I need to be strong
don't tell me to keep moving on
don't act as if the tears I cry are a sign of weakness
you wouldn't understand why
don't tell me I need to be there for everyone else
I matter too, I'm going through hell

my heart is breaking, I'm saying goodbye
my life changed forever, you can't comprehend how
there's a hole in my heart
a knot in my stomach and my throat is choked up
I won't pretend just to make you feel better
this isn't something time will heal

I am allowed to feel
I am allowed to cry
I am allowed to shout, to wonder why
I am allowed to be there, just for me
I am allowed to grieve in a way that sets me free

-Lizzy in words-

Obey

Wrung feelings drop
But surely boomerang back
Like hopeful puppies
But just as naive

-Greg Oman-

, 434One More Time

Sometimes she sit nearby the window
Glancing at the stars and moon
Wishing deeply as always
He was with her
Holding her hand, looking at her
Just one more time

There is one she belongs to
But someone else she long for
Her heart filled with him to the brim
Until the day they both part ways
She wishes it to be one more time

The tender smiles and caresses
In between the warmth of his embraces
The sweet whispers of nothingness
The place she loved the most
One more time just one more time

-Aliya Ameer-

Missing You

Like a satin pillow
Lush and full of lavender
Memories of you are fragrant and deep
Softly cradling my aching head
Let me sleep in peace
Dreaming of what was

-L. Wright-

Her

We were at different stages of life.
Mine was just beginning but yours was about to end.
What would I have changed if I had known?
Too much has happened for me to ignore that feeling I had for you.
Maybe I was your best friend but for me,
you were so much more.
We cried together,
shared our darkest secrets.
If I'm honest
you saved my life.
To go on any longer would have been a miracle.
People cursing my name right to my face,
clawing at my humanity.
labelling me worthless.
You shone above the cruel words
and carried me with you.
Maybe it would be different if you were still around.
But oh how I loved every second I spent with you.
I always wonder if you even felt the same.

-Amy Littleford-

Place Me In The Sun

Place me in the sun and let me stay there. I'll reminisce in the warmth, soaking in hopeful clarity. I don't mind the rain every now and then, it cleanses me. This too shall pass like everything in life always does, even the things we wanted to stay.

-Stacy Evans B-

The Architect

There's a sadness that comes with nostalgia.
As you come to realise
The world you once knew is no more,
Colours run like paintings left in rain
Like chalk lines drawn on pavements
In places you spent your youth,
Now paved over in the name of progress.

The boy you were looked back
Over his shoulder to wave at companions
Looked back a man growing grey,
As grey as the world had become in between,
Perhaps still a prism of colour can still be glimpsed,
As light passes fading in the tears
On his cheeks and the memories
Of the lost boys he used to know.

In the end we all grow up.
We, Peter Pans, peter out
Grow old, bed and blanket
Ourselves with white lemon peel to rot,
The curse of failing flesh
Is all but inevitable,
yet.

It needn't have come
To the washed-out grey
That crept into our hair,
Our faces, our eyes,
Our souls.

The colour ran but we could always run with it,
The past passed as we looked behind us for it
But we could always catch up,
The lost boys could always be found.

Aye, there's a sadness that comes with nostalgia
When you come to understand,
The loneliest feeling is
Knowing you are the architect
Of your own lost youth.

And suddenly it is too late.

-Greg Rowan Shearer-

Walk-About

Time to go a walk-about
Along the song lines
Searching for truth
And seeking you
Disappearing
Into the wild
Midst the silence
Listening
For the melodic
Soft voice of you
The undiscovered beckons
To doubting sojourners
Destined to wait for
The return of you

-Mark Wayne-

Andrew

Many months have passed
since his last breath was taken.
His death by another,
so senseless and cruel.
The pain of such loss
leaving deep wounds within us,
in all those who love him
and hold him so close.
Tears endlessly falling
from eyes that don't see him,
apart from the images
captured in life.
All strength to my sister,
her husband and daughters.
To all those whose heart aches
with the missing of him.

-Kathy Coutts-

Let Me Be Soil

Dear Earth,
Please take this pain from my soul.
Refresh it, reuse it.

In your delicate hands
Decaying things again grow.
Take this hurt,
Help me let go.

-Austie M. Baird-

Soul Spot

shivers run down my spine
as a whisper fills my ear
my body finally asleep
when your soul is coming near
no eerie feelings, but those of peace
as your arms are holding me
I hug you tight and say 'I miss you'
and you tell me 'I know my dear'
I try to hold on as long as I can
to this moment of feeling you here
but you have to go back
so you have to let go
and my body awakens from its sleep
while tears fill my eyes I feel a little shaken
for no measure of time is long enough
in the place where our two souls meet

-Lizzy in words-

Hollow

One thing I've learned is that life is far too short to hold back your feelings.
If you love someone, let them know before it's too late.

As we sat up on that High Line, watching the sun set over the Hudson River,
my hand in yours, my head on your shoulder, I was ready to tell you.
But as you turned to look at me with those beautiful eyes and loving smile,
the words caught in the hollow of my throat and I choked.
Rendered speechless, I let the moment pass –
like so many before it, and so many after…

And now my hollow chest aches for just one more moment with you, to set those words free and make sure you knew how much you meant to me.

I wonder – Can you hear me in the afterlife?

-Whiskey + Empathy-

Waves

sadness was a wave
in which she had been drowning
trying to teach herself how to surf
towards a silver lining

-Lizzy in words-

Fallacy of Memories

I remember you
As you were before
You went away
Not how you
Would look today if
You had stayed
An image in the
Fallacy of memories
My mind portrays

-Mark Wayne-

A Picture of Us

I had to take our picture off the wall.
I hid it away for another day.
A day when I am ready to embrace the pain.
Today is not that day.
I never thought I could miss someone like I miss you.
Our memories are branded on the inside of my brain.
I am trying to hold onto them.
I promise.
But as the years go by
certain parts seem to fade.
All I am left with is your beautiful face.
A picture only captured by my eyes.

-Amy Littleford-

Birthday

it's a day of remembrance
the day of my birth
the day on which you brought me
upon this earth
the first day I saw you
and felt the touch of your skin
that first day we met
the moment it would all begin
a journey through all life had to share
with beauty and tears
nothing was spared
yet today also marks remembering a loss
of moments past, no future ahead
so how can today be about me
when all I can think of
is your seat staying empty
a void that can never be filled
I suppose I should celebrate
your very first kiss
forever lingering on my skin
I shall celebrate
breathing your love in

-Lizzy in words-

Till Death Do Us Part

You never told me
About this
He said

She only stared and
Slowly shook
Her head

Till death do us
Part was all
She said

-Mark Wayne-

Pain

Living with a heavy heart
like the heavy clouds on sky
relieving by letting go little water
like the rain pouring down...

-Aliya Ameer-

Things My Nonno Taught Me.

1. Never leave ginger nuts in the tin with other biscuits otherwise they all taste like ginger nuts.

2. Best sandwich in the world is a toasted Italian loaf, with parmesan roasted on it, pepper and crushed pecorino on top, rocket and corned beef.

3. Punch fascists in the face before they kill the people you love.

4. Women are always right unless they aren't.

5. Don't smoke a sigaretta to the wid that's what kills people.

6. Never be ashamed of who you are even when it could kill you.

7. If it feels right then it's probably right and if it's wrong, then laugh.

8. A sense of humour will keep you alive longer than any medicine.

9. Square sausage and plum tomatoes are a delicacy whether you're in work or the workhouse.

10. If you can read your weight in books you don't need an education.

11. The shirt on your back is rarely worth the person you could hand it to.

12. No matter what it is, it is what it is, it either passes, or you enjoy it while you can.

13. Never be afraid of the gutter, you'll never know how close you are to walking in it or waking in it.

14. If you've got a garden, then grow fruit.

15. If you're going to greet then make sure it's worth greeting about.

16. Perry Como will always be a star.

17. Don't be feart to talk to people whether it's a lassie standing herself or a man in front of a crowd.

18. Treat everyone as an equal but some of them a bit better.

19. Never drink alone.

20. La casa é dove si trova il cuore.

21. Love isn't one sided even when someone is gone.

-Greg Rowan Shearer-

Missing

you left an imprint on my soul
the very day we met
you took a part of me away
the very day you left

-Lizzy in words-

Blossom

if tears could blossom into flowers
I'd be walking through a garden
of the most beautiful kind
where new scents erupt
with every drop touching the soil
growing, not from weakness
but from being too strong
moving with the winds of the world
rooted and nurtured
yet time to let be
every step moving forward
setting tears free

-Lizzy in words-

The Oceans Between Us

entire oceans
between us
but still
my heart is compelled
to you
my soul illuminates
at the thought
of you

you are everything
and nothing
at once

-Abi Hayes-

Love of God

Missing your love
With the
Love of God
So close
At hand
It seems
Sacrilegious
However
I think He
Understands

-Mark Wayne-

Heavenly Blinders

I've come to believe
That heaven's eyes
Do not watch
As on earth we weep.

For how could those angels sweet
Enjoy the fruits of their toiled labors,
If witnessing
The torn and tortured souls
Their departures did leave?

No, I fear they see us not.
For their own safe keeping,
Peace to keep.

-Austie M. Baird-

Pray for Us

Let's start with a mystery
Unknowing but wanting to know
Where the curious frolic
And we begin to know comfort;
Comfort in the moment of knowing
Worries flee to be free
But with the corner's glance
A shadow does creep
And we focus on that
And nothing else
Because perfection is a funny thing
And we can't have a shadow in the midst
In the mist-
Looming
Dooming
But alas, at least for some
We know the sum
The shadow is the relief
Let's end without misery

-Greg Oman-

Heartbeat

After all this time
I still hear your heartbeat
In every dream
And memory of you

-Mark Wayne-

Homesick

You were my
first home

my lighthouse

a harbour
for my soul
to stay

so is it
any wonder
that day after
day
after
day

I still feel
a little bit

homesick

-Abi Hayes-

Maybe...

May be it would have been a little more fun exploring places with you by my side
May be the food would have appealed to the taste buds a little more along with you
May be the people I meet appeared a little more interesting with your perspectives added,
May be the diverse cultures a little more unique with your vision shared,
May be the opinion on world affairs more spirited with you to debate with, May be the problems a little less big with your support,
May be the hills and clouds would have looked a little more prettier holding your hands,
May be the nature would have seemed a little more majestical with your beauty to compare with
Maybe the temples, mosques and churches would have felt a little more divine,
your love
May be I could have experienced life a little bit more filled with

Living alone is fine, but
May be with you it would have been better

- *Vivek*

Begin Again

Decades of joy
Now gone and buried
Limestone and wreaths hold tribute
The lilies droop and the mourners recede
"Gone but not forgotten" seems so trite
Your love planted courage
Sprouting here is hope
Now a beginning

-L. Wright-

Moving Forward

I'm starting to feel again
and it breaks my heart
for not sharing it with you

every step through life without you
will always be one too many
so what good can these feelings do

-Lizzy in words-

Inheritance

I inherited from you
A breast so full of burden,
This heart you had,
Half drowned in cheap drink
Mottled from cigarette ash,
Wholly stained by indigo bruises
And stitched with self-inflicted scars
Yet, still it beats on.

You lay to be swallowed up
By cold earth and freakish things
That feast on flesh and shun light,
We stood around a man-made gullet
Waiting to be swallowed up by grief
That never came,
We had mourned you long before this.

Not that we didn't weep or care
We did, more than you knew
But like saying goodbye
To lost weight
That was part of us once,
We were glad to see you go.

Not you, the burden
Shaped like the man you had become,
Who called me by my father's name
Who told his son to get to fuck
Who asked every day,
Where Betty was.

Even though he had held
Her hand as she slipped
Beyond the gentle touch of his fingertips
Like a snowflake held in warm hands.

She so precious, so delicate, so pristine white
The way I remember her hair to be
Melted and passed into memory.

And memories now elusive mysteries
A vague mist of recall and cigarette smoke
Knowing what dementia is,
I still say you went mad with grief.

After a time, one morning I awoke
And felt something as
Dawn broke back the shadow,
Not for first or second time,
The world stirred again.

Sunshine yellow warmth crept
Across this weary sons' skin
Until the black blues pain
Finally faded.

That feeling you never came to know.
It was healing.

-Greg Rowan Shearer-

Dig

i have known so many people
with shovels for hands.
you are not the first.
so, please, do not be ashamed.
i know you cannot help yourself,
and i know i cannot stop you
once you begin to dig a hole.
dig a ditch.
dig a grave.
dig a tunnel
into the depths of despair.
dig yourself deeper
and deeper
until disaster
has made a home out of you.
but, trust
that on the days
when you do not have the strength
to dig yourself
out,
i will come.

i will come
devoted and determined.
with white knuckles
and dirt-caked fingernails.
i will dig
to bring you back
from the darkness.
because some days
my hands
look a lot like shovels, too.

some days
i find dirt in my ears,
a pounding in my skull.
some days,
when i am neck deep and desperate for air,
i find that my arms
are suddenly more earthworm than pickaxe.
all the muscle dissolved into ache.
some days,
all i can hope for
is someone to haul me out.

so when i say,
i understand,
what i mean to say is,
i know well the way sorrow
can taste like soil on the tongue.
the way it can slide gritty down the throat.
settle like a graveyard in the chest.

when i say
i am not afraid
to get my hands dirty,
what i mean to say is,
i love you.
what i mean to say is,
i will not let you
be buried alive.

-Emily May Portillo

Unicorns and Etta

There was nothing extraordinary about that night.
We were in the kitchen, cleaning up after dinner, just talking.
Smokey music softly playing from the other room.

I don't even remember what I was saying, but the way he was
suddenly staring at me froze me in my tracks.
I looked around – clearly, I was missing something.

Then, out of nowhere, eyes sparkling, he called me a unicorn.
I started to laugh, but he pulled me into his arms and silenced me,
saying, "You're a Goddamned fucking Unicorn. Where
have you been?!"

Cradling me tighter into his embrace, he kissed the top of my head
and we began to sway to the music.

And now every time I hear Etta James' 'A Sunday Kinda Love'
I think of him – and unicorns – and smile.

-Whiskey + Empathy-

Cleansing Water

I know my heart is healing
when my ears, once again, seek out music
and my voice starts to sing on its own
hurt washed away by cleansing water
like the sun after the storm

- Lizzy in words-

Lucretius

so sensed the wind,

as it pushed,
as it pulled,

as a face prepared,
a scream, a dream,
a tear that paired,

water and air,
drowning, saving,
dust, atoms, in,

out from lungs,
out, this heart,
out, out, warm,
in wind,

living,
captured, freed,
they are, I am,
dust, hope, out,

without form now,
dispersed, a universe,
in verse,
from whence, from when,

eternal, an ether,
in love,
again.

-J. Savarese-

You Are the Moon

I see you in the moon
You were more than a life taken too soon
More than a watercolor painting
Not protected enough against the nights of raining
You were my comfort blanket against fear
Loved filled kisses for the tears
A beating heart waiting by the door
That doesn't wait anymore
I feel guilty for being adjusted to the empty space in my bed
That your voice is fading till I forget
I feel disgusted that I have to hear it
To be reminded
Time is struggling to heal me
Because I'm fighting it, like it will be undone easily
How is it that I'm missing you so bad
Yet am being adjusted to live without what we had
I miss everything even your snoring
And the need for loving without warning
I miss you with every breath I take
I'm waiting for myself to break
Utterly and completely
But you loved me unconditionally
I carry you with me
I see you in the moon
You are the moon
You continue to bright up my darkest night
So I'll try not to fight
And let time heal me
Till I'm back to the heart that you once loved unconditionally

-Mari Antoinette-

Hope

I had a revival today. I was the only one there. I sang a hymn of repentance for my regrets, then asked myself for forgiveness. I had always read that God did not give us a spirit of timidity, because I've been letting these mortal voices drown out my truth. I kept my uniqueness in the cupboard for a rainy day. I've always fought the good fight, but mostly for others, forgetting that I never had my own back, but today will be different, because I awoke to an awakening, and I started to breathe for myself. Now I'm letting my soul dance to a new song called liberation.

-Stacy Evans Brown-

Last Kiss

Here's the thing about kisses…
You'll always remember the first,
and you'll always remember the last.

But you'll never have another first or last kiss with the same person.
When you can look back and remember your second, tenth, even your fifty-first kiss – the way their lips felt on yours, the way you indulged in their scent as your tongues slowly danced a song only the two of you heard –
You'll know that was something magical.
So make sure you take the time to remember each kiss you share; engage all your senses.
Because you never know when your last kiss,
will be your last.

-Whiskey + Empathy

The Birds are in The Garden

The birds are in the garden
and they have begun to sing.
The washing is off the line
and the kettle is boiling.

The little dog has run outside
and trotted out the gate.
Normally he'd go with his leash,
but this time he couldn't wait.

The pictures have been taken out
and are propped up again.
Before they caused discomfort,
but now they help memories remain.

The birds are in the garden,
and they have begun to sing.
'This is where you belong,'
I can hear them whispering.

- Jamie Rhiannon Fehribach-

Connected

there's a little string connecting us
crossing barriers of space and time
woven out of love
connecting your soul with mine

-Lizzy in words-

Hope

Standing alone in thoughts
Gazing the early morning
Rays weaving through the sky
Lightening up the surroundings
Arising for a new horizon
Peeking over the hills
The orange thread of light
As if giving the hope
As inexpressibly beautiful
The soft touch of rays
Squeezing through the clouds
Start afresh as the sun reborns

-Aliya Ameer-

You Make Me Question

You make me question existence itself,
You make me wonder if there is a god
Who sent you down to earth for me,
You make me want to see what love tastes like
To see whether it is bitter or sweet,
You make me want to be a better person
To be the best version of myself for you,
You make me see the light even in the darkest of times.

-Starr-

This Piece is For You

For the you who lies on the bathroom floor, face soaked and also crusted with new and old tears. Eyes red and puffy and long since should have gone dry yet continue to pour for his. You miss him, I know. And this is to tell you that it's okay to miss him, you don't have to get over it or move on right now. Let yourself feel, let yourself cry, let your heart break. He was a part of your life for what feels like a fleeting moment but also eternity and that shit takes time to process and recover from. Take as much time as you need my darling. But remember, you survived without him before and you will survive without him after. You are the moon, whole. You have everything you need inside you but for now, mourn. It is okay to mourn the loss of someone who was special. Someone who changed your life and gave you so many new feelings and experiences. Grieve for the part of your heart that feels like it was torn from your chest. You are valid and worth it and beautiful from the inside out. And you will find someone else who makes you feel all kinds of butterflies. He was not the only one.

-Michelle Perkins-

Oh Young Heart

Your heart is small because you're young
so precious that you are
When Grandma passed away last year
she became an eternal star

Your heart is small because you're young
but know that as it grows
A part of Grandma lives inside
blooming like a rose

Your heart is small because you're young
and though it misses her dearly
Feel the emotions where
Grandma's love will whisper clearly

Your heart is small because you're young
it's storing up love and healing
Grandma will be with us always
the brightest star in the sky appealing

-Linda Lokhee-

Coming Alive

Losing you
Inspired life in me

-Nikki C Mercer-

Why Did You Have To Go So Early?

Dearest Grandma,

The heart breathed its last and it left a hundred other hearts broken. Memories flashed and vanished like shooting stars bringing endless tears. They weren't merely tears of sorries and condolences, but tears of gratitude, thank-you notes, and regrets. As a personification of patience, tolerance, compassion, joy and placidity, you showered unconditional love upon all of us in your own inimitable style.

We take the air we breathe and the water we drink for granted and so did we take the love you showered on us. You loved us all too much, more than what all of us deserved, and the absence of it with your sudden departure has, hit us all very hard.

Your smile was poise. Your palms were soft. Your eyes were serene. A simple cotton saree was your haute couture. And you were so beautiful, both on the outside and within.

The coffee you brewed on Sunday afternoons, when we visited to talk about the week before, the week ahead, stories, music, and about everything we generally didn't talk to people about, were filled not just with milk, sugar and decoction but with your affection and warmth.

You believed in us and you gave us immense moral support for all our academic and music endeavors. You clarified our silly doubts over phone. You called us every day just to hear our voices. You asked us if we were doing fine as a routine over phone. We know it's too late to tell you, but 'Thank you' for all that, Grandma. On the other hand, we are sorry if we didn't respond properly, when we had a test the next day or, just felt a little tired to talk, or was engrossed in watching a TV show. We are sorry; we didn't send a recording of the song you had asked for. We're sorry we didn't give you a manicure. We're sorry; we didn't get the biscuits you wanted and we're sorry we didn't change the bedspreads the week before you passed on.

You gave us strength. You taught us determination. You spread positivity. And you submerged us in the ocean of happiness. We have no words to express what you meant to us and what you mean to us even more now.

You have given us memories to cherish, values to embrace and most importantly a part of you as a caring and a loving mother. Thank you very much, Patti!

Lots of love,
Your grandchildren

-Harshitha Satish-

You

your face is captured in my memory
your love is written on my heart

-Brianne Reilly-

He Is Bitter Sweet

He is bitter sweet,
He makes me happy
But can make me cry a river
Just by looking away,
He makes me want to scream in agony
Yet
Thank god for sending me this angel,
His words are a trigger only he knows how to use,
He can shoot me down or lift me up in a second,
And the sad part is
That
I'd let him
Do anything
And I's still belong to him
For eternity.

-Starr-

Shadows

Though you're shattered, bruised
and holes are in your heart
Let me be the one
to place the pieces
back together again

Because sweetheart
your light still shines
through those holes and
I can see your goodness

-Linda Lokhee-

Becoming Whole

You can't be strong all the time.
Sometimes you just have to break down
in order to put yourself back together again.
This is an essential part of the growth process.
Let yourself fall apart.
With every falling tear,
feel yourself becoming lighter
as you let go of all the pain.
Then when you are ready,
pick yourself back up
piece by piece,
and put yourself back together again.
Even if it seems like there are pieces of you missing now,
just allow yourself the time to heal
and surrender to the knowing
that you will become whole again.

-Angela Marie Niemiec-

Another Chance

when light was gone
and emptiness encompassed

you skipped river stones
across the ocean of my heart

I felt ripples of love form
and settle deep in my soul

- Linda Lokhee-

Falling

I'm standing at the edge
looking back at everything I have
everything I had and everything I wanted
a life weighing me down
I can feel the itch between my shoulders
wings wanting to break through
one step forward is all it takes
I close my eyes, say one last prayer
'teach me how to spread my wings, teach me how to fly'
before my feet slip off the edge
falling into the abyss

a mist surrounding me
voices so pure calling me
did I fall to pieces
am I still alive
I am floating, I feel free
there's a force surrounding me
a light too bright for eyes to bear
glimpses of shimmering white and gold
a strength I never felt before
peace and love beyond all measure
no more weight upon my shoulders
only wings lifting me up
my soul is free
I'm home
I'm me

-Lizzy in words-

Resilience

do not be afraid
of being left behind.
not of solitude.
not of loss.

i have seen homes
made of discarded daisies
and leftover love.
lives rebuilt
on foundations of mist
and memories.

you would be amazed
by what you can create
with nothing more
than scraps,
and hope,
and a heart
willing to dirty its hands.

-Emily May Portillo-

Long Way Home

Why did you die?
Why aren't you here?
I'm scared all the time,
But you're not there
Not there to smile
And make me brave
Not there at all
Just make-believe
I share my secrets
But there's no reply
No arms to hold me
When I cry
I'm lonely and small
But the oldest of all
I have to be the grown up now
But I'm too small, I don't know how
Mum needs me to help
But it isn't fair
Can't I just be a kid?
Why aren't you here?
I'm finishing school now
I'll have a job soon enough
I'm not mad anymore
But I still find it tough
I wish you were able to tell me
You're proud of who I am
I wish you could see me now
Tell me I'm becoming a man
I've travelled the world now
I have a home of my own
With my wife and children
My eldest is all grown
I sometimes have moments
Where I'm quiet and sad

Moments when I wonder
What life would've been with you Dad
Then I stare at these young faces
And you look back at me smiling
You're no longer gone
But I still feel like crying
They're happy tears now
Not realising back then
That I'd look at my children and see you in them.

-Jason Morgan-

Seeds of Spring

This life,
in search of love,
a vast and yearning world.

These skies,
without my dove,
no dreams, no wings unfurled.

Death,
the flowers hold,
what never could I give.

Spring,
a dream foretold,
your seeds in mine,

now live.

-J. Savarese-

Happy Birthday – I Miss You

A sliver of morning light streams in, gently waking me.
I roll over to check my phone for the time,
but all I see is my calendar notification.

As if I need a reminder...
Today is the day we should be celebrating your existence, another year of life.
Instead, a tsunami of memories floods my brain – every moment shared,
every emotion felt with you, washes over me.

I miss your laugh; your smile; your arms around me; your kiss.
I miss the way you would caress the side of my face;
the way I would drown in the depths of your enamored gaze.
I miss the way you could make me feel like the only girl in the world,
even though the line was out the door.
I miss the sense of peace and comfort I felt in your presence;
the way you made everyone feel special, including me.
I miss... you.

And so now today, I'll smoke a cigar in your honor.
Now, today is about remembering you, celebrating the life you lived,
and giving gratitude for the part of that life you so lovingly shared with me.

Thank you for everything, Sailor... Happy Birthday…

-Whiskey + Empathy-

Rescued

i can't do this on my own
I said when you'd gone
the day i lost my fire
my flame
my sun
you don't have to
they whispered
words sparking with magic
igniting the furnace once
burned
to
ashes
and they gathered shattered parts
broken fragments of my heart
and pieced them back together
shard
by
shard.

-Abi Hayes-

Memories

A smile on your face or a tear drop on your eyes,
memories can take various shapes

- Vivek-

Dear Daddy

What do I do with these memories?
That I can't touch or see...but only feel?
When I wanted you to walk me down the aisle?
Or be there for the birth of my child?

What do I do with these memories?
In so many scenarios, I must wonder what you would say or do?
What advice would you offer, what steps shall I choose?

I only have memories, stories and pictures.
Pictures, stories and memories.
Those are the only times that I could ever see you again.

As a child it was hard.
As an adult I realize that I miss you more and more.
I could burst out into tears because, you'll never walk through that door.

If you were here, I can't say what our status would have been.
But a video of us dancing is locked into my memory.
I cherish your words to me.
You said, "No one is gonna love you, like I love you."

I believe it to be true, it's tattooed on my heart,
& inked into the eternity of my spirit.
My soul will always feel it.
For you are forever alive in my heart.

I love you too, Dad!

- Jereni-Sol-

Learning to be Whole

A part of me used to hate you
For letting the addiction take you captive
& demanding the ransom of my childhood
But as I got older, I started to understand you
I know now how easily life can break you down
& make you feel unrepairable

As kids, we forget that our parents lived lives before us
They were not always so self-less and all-knowing
& sometimes they can't escape the demons they buried
before we became part of their world

I forgave my dad a long time ago
Because he did the best he could in teaching me to be whole
Even when he was so broken
I thought for a while that his death would break me
Even if it was years later
Just like his dad's death broke him
But instead, it made me stronger
& for that I know he is proud

-Erica Rolston [EDR]-

Tender

Void snatches boy,
while mother and father
watch.

Unable to prevent,
only able to mourn
the loss.

Pain of having pictures
past, with no chance
for future.

A love statuesque in
it's nature begins
to decay.

Inevitably, it falters
under the weight
of child gone.

Little sister weeps,
processes, cold
and alone.

Parents have all
but forgotten
little girl.

The loss of son
makes them
neglect...

s h i n e .

So daughter is left
to fend for herself
in shadow.

But she is strong,
because she
speaks to
brother
daily.

He comforts her
from the lands,
skies and seas
beyond.

Laughs with her,
watches her grow,
till she plays with
child of her own.

But he can't help

c r y i n g .

Not for his loss of life,
impact on parents
or initial loneliness
of little sister.

No, he cries
because he has
a nephew.

One with
heart of mother,
will of father,
spirit of sister
and his n a m e .

A dead child
memorialized
in the love
of a living boy.

A tenderness unexpected,
proving that even the
dead may w e e p .

-Gabriel Rodriguez-

The Stages of Coping

Fear is a quality we all possess,
And tend to leave as quite a mess.
Here is my tale to unveil
About loss and emotional bail.

(Regression)
When I was a child, very sweet and mild,
It did not matter what life bared.
So when it causes my mind to run wild,
I think back to how I previously cared.

(Repression)
But sometimes I just want to forget about it all,
Run with the wind, pretend, and stand tall.
If I do that, my mind won't act like a brat,
But perhaps I won't ever change my habitat.

(Reaction Formation)
I like to play tricks on my surroundings,
Manipulate them instead of drowning.
Instead of saying what I feel,
Indicate the opposite, and cause others to reel.

(Projection)
But what if I like this feeling of control?
Hoard onto others let's make that my goal.
Who says these problems are my own?
It's your own, his own, her own, to disown.

(Rationalization)
Maybe I should come back to my own self.
Justify my reasoning, trick my mind's elf.
I'll reach a logical conclusion for my horrors,
Instead of creating a swarm of my mourners.

(Displacement)
WAIT! I still have a way to blame others.
I'll pick on those less aggressive, see what it stirs.
Then I can let go of myself, read their reactions,
And divide everything further into its factions.

(Sublimation)
I still can't find the answers to my problems,
So I will create my future in different realms.
I'll channel my hurt into a passion-
And never retire this classic I fashioned.

-Diya Nijhawan-

True Friendship Never Dies

I still think of you my friend
and reminisce on fun times gone by
Laughing at your silly jokes
True friendship not needed to simplify

And when That News came
seems I'd known you a lifetime
Your family and mine so close
All our lives entwined

The disease was unexpected
paired with a shock so cruel
All our rage at first
towards it was our fuel

No reason for the attack
on your lungs that were so young
So quickly you fell victim
Down life's ladder unwillingly swung

You left way too soon
and our hearts broke that day
The pieces of us here
left to continue your ray

Time has ticked by
yet you're not in the past
You're here in our memories
still alive, forever to last

I hear you in your son's laugh
I see you in your daughter's eyes
A flash of what we shared
sometimes takes me by surprise

True friendship never dies
perhaps now it's put on hold
You, forever young
while we're left to grow old

You're thought of often and
hearts have a healing design
Oh how I wish that cancer
was just a simple star sign

-Linda Lokhee-

Overcome

from my deepest low
once again
You help me rise
how majestic
Your love
moving mountains
before my feet
creating wonders
before my eyes

-Lizzy in words-

Dear Betty

I knew you were dying. I began preparing. I told my mind that you would physically leave: no more two hour phone calls, no more dinners at the Mexican restaurant we liked to frequent, no more friendship. I told myself this. I was prepared.

Then I saw you in your coffin, again my mind told me you were in a better place. You finally attained peace. But my heart broke anyway, into millions of pieces. It has not been mended since.

It has been eleven years, and I have not visited your grave. I have yet to bring you flowers and I have yet to find a friend as kind as you. You cared about me, you loved me and I you. You were always there for me, never disappointing me. You set the bar extremely high. Honestly, I will never again have a friend like you.

I thought that was awful and sad. I never realized how lucky I was to have known you, to have called you my friend. You were a part of my life for ten years, now I realize what a gift that is.

I know you are still here, I've felt your presence so many times. And I smile. Someday, when the time is right, I will meet you again. My only hope is that you will know it is me.

Love always,

-Brianne Bowman-

Letter I'll Never Send

One year later...
I can still hear your voice;
Both your mischievous chuckle and roaring laugh.
Still remember the feel of our last kiss, and all the ones that came before.

Memories we created out of moments shared together, play like reels of tape in my mind.
And that bitter cold night...

The first gig I'd missed in almost a year.
I should've been there. I would've been with you.
Like everyone else, I chastised myself, thinking I could've done something, somehow helped.
But the truth is, there was nothing anyone could have done.

So, I learned to find solace in the fact that my last memory with you is of an amazing evening we enjoyed,
and not you dying on me.
And all those wonderful moments we had,
everything you taught me,
all the confidence you instilled by always believing in me –
I am blessed for knowing you and the time we shared.
There were so many things we planned to do together that will never happen;
So many things I wanted to say that I'll never get the chance to tell you.

So I write these letters that I cannot send, and whisper the words aloud,
in hopes you will hear what I wish to believe you already knew...

-Whiskey + Empathy-

Capturing Fireflies

I captured my memories of you,
and placed them inside a glass jar.
Holding it close and so none could dare escape,
I screwed on the lid twisting it as tightly as I could.
Like the fireflies we had captured when we were young,
each memory flew innocently around inside the jar.
Upon rising the next morn, I came to find,
inside the jar, each memory was dead from lack of air.
Utter despair filled my heart not one memory was left.
I resolved that I could and would do better,
so eagerly I set about capturing more.

Into the glass jar, I placed each one and again
screwed down the lid, this time tighter than before.
Believing I had learned a hard lesson in life,
I punched holes in the top so air would enter in,
believing the memories would now never die.
I watched them flutter so happily about,
which brought an ever present smile to my face.
Until, eventually I dozed in this contented place.

I woke many hours later in the early evening.
I looked for the memories to remind me of you
but the jar I held was now empty and cold.
Unscrewing the lid, I could find nothing there.
I sighed deeply, realizing that the holes must have
been too big, allowing each memory to escape.
I could not ever hold them I thought,
as I sat clasping the jar with clenched fists.

The evening began to fade as the dark curtain
of night began to fall covering the land.
My hands still gripped tightly to the empty jar,
my heart void of anything, feeling nothing.
The darkness smothered the forgotten light of day.
Finally, I dared to move and looking up over my head,
I was astounded by the sight before me.

A million twinkling lights, each a single memory of you
shone white hot against the dark canvas of night.
As each memory flooded back in wave after wave,
I distinctly and clearly remembered this one.
How we ran and laughed capturing fireflies,
without a care in the world, when we were young.

-Mark Wayne-

Someday Without Crying

It's natural to wonder
how you'll get through the hardest days ahead,
when the storm clouds cover so dark,
your skies feel black and the light is no more.
It's no wonder you'll turn your back
on those who tell you to smile,
and want you to get better,
as if they even know what you are going through,
but they do.
They know you'll regain your strength.
It won't happen overnight, or even in a day.
There will be times your nearly mended wounds
will be ripped wide open again,
but eventually scars will cover those
and someday,
just someday,
you'll be able to tell your story
without crying.

-Angela Marie Niemiec-

A Lonely Road

down this rabbit hole I run
lost in the muted colors of the sun
haunted by a past that came undone
the future lies unopened before me
a present wrapped in pretty bows

inside the box waits
unknown stories of fate
my destiny was denied
rebuilt again with leftovers
my anger builds to be left alone
a hand slipped away taking with it the dreams of youth
to start again is now so real
to feel again despite the pain
letting go of a suitcase of dreams
two worlds clamor for my attention

one in front, one from behind
both screaming at the top of their lungs
two lives; one completely undone, one only begun
lost within feelings I can't put away
what to do, what to say

happiness is a lonely road
walking away from the known
letting go it makes me sad putting it behind
for better things lie ahead
even if the eyes can't see

what is around the next bend
trusting in unspoken promises
a future of dreams sleep fitfully
sometime soon but for now I smile
for I know I will see you again

-Mark Wayne-

Keep Living

There will be days,
When grey is your color
-keep living.

There will be moments,
That weigh your shoulders to the ground
-keep living.

There will be darkness,
When all you seek is light
-keep living.

There will be pain,
Locked behind silent eyes
-keep living.

There will be moments,
When fingers reach and come up empty
-keep living.

There will be a time,
When all feels right
-keep fucking living.

-Austie M. Baird-

You Come To Me

You come to me
evoking the color green
wafting on a springtime breeze
Carried on the notes of blue
an elegy that speaks of you
You are the warmth in yellow
rays of summer sunlight
The silver flash of lightning
that illuminates darkened stormy skies
You are the orange and gold
in crisp autumn leaves
and the winter white of falling snow
You are the red that seeps
with every beat from my broken heart.

-Carrie Fossier-

Let the Underdogs Arise

Let the underdogs arise. Pick up your confidence and light it on fire. Let the world announce its new heroes. Let your silenced voices be heard again, then gain strength from knowing your worth.

-Stacy Evans Brown-

On Loss

We talk about loss when someone dies
Our heart broken, we breathe in sighs.
Yet we should think of, in the main,
what they taught us, what we gained.

We dress in black, we do not smile.
We don't socialise for a while.
Yet what we should do is celebrate
The life of those who are now 'late'.

We are left all void and alone
An empty heart an empty home.
Yet we should just fill the space
With the joy we found in their face

We torture ourselves thinking
Regretting, our hearts sinking
Instead, awake, smile and ponder
They are not far, just yonder.

'Time heals', you keep on hearing.
Loneliness you are fearing.
Instead, know that they live with you
While you live, they live too.

-Odette Millar-

Never Alone

did I not tell you I would be there till the end
did I not promise to wrap my arms around you
oh my love, how close I'm holding you
I still walk beside you, never letting go
this end you saw, was my new beginning
my way back home
oh my sweet girl, my wings shine bright
I can see your pain
talk to me like you always did
I'm here with you beyond the end
waiting till we meet again
until it's time for you to journey
to this place that you call home
even in a million years
you are never alone

-Lizzy in words-

Through My Tragedy

Through my tragedy, I help out hope. Amidst the sorry, I felt the coming peace. Inside the darkness and pain of life, I patiently endured, knowing that no matter what may come, the light would always find its way back to me.

-Stacy Evens B.-

Whiskey, Empathy, and the 12 Apostles: Saint Peter

His eyes glinted with genuine admiration
whenever I was in his presence.
My heart filled with joy and my soul felt light
whenever he was in mine.

Every moment we shared exuberating, and filled with a lust for life.

There was a natural ease when we were together...
Conversation flowed as easily as champagne on New Year's Eve;
Any silence devoid of awkwardness;
And oh how that man could make me laugh!

Watching the sun set over the Hudson River,
walking the boardwalk down the shore,
dancing in the middle of the street,
admiring the night sky, cooking together,
car rides home holding hands,
even just lying in bed
listening to music,
I felt completely at peace.
A sense of comfort I had never known.

I'll always cherish the time I had with him.
He made me a better woman.

-Whiskey + Empathy-

Never Really Gone

You think about that day you hear the news.
Your stomach drops like you're falling a thousand feet.
The unfathomable feeling that you will never see them again,
but no one is ever truly gone.

You hear a note of their laughter in a relative's chuckle.
You see a glimpse of their smile,
a twinkle from their eye in another's.

It sparks those cheerful memories,
but you grieve.
You long for the past,
to have the time all over again,
and relive those memories.

You want to the world stop for going on without them,
But it doesn't.
You feel like screaming
'how can people keep going on like nothing has happened?'
How can they just disappear?
like a jigsaw with missing pieces that you never find,
and never be complete again.

But people who are no longer in your life
have a permanence to your soul,
even if it is a little spec.
The wisdom that they have given you,
the mannerisms you have adopted,
or a life lesson you've never forgotten.

They make up the fibres of the person you are.
And you should be so proud to take them with you on your own journey.
Thank them for having the absolute pleasure for being a part of theirs,
And cherish the blessing of everything they have given you.

They are with you every step of the way,
in spirit, living on with you,
part of you.
They will never leave you....

-Fay Collins-

Deep Waters

if the light
of giving gets
consummated
by treachery,
don't stop giving!
the darkness
is volatile,
it could flow
either ways,
let the
shallow side
be theirs,
deep waters
never fall short.

-Alkesha Chaudhary-

The Sky Is Soft

The sky is soft
And blue
But also pink
And peach
And purple
All stretched across
The horizon
All I can see
As the sun goes down
Is your face
Glistening
Up in the clouds
I miss you
But you're still here
Gazing over me
Warming me
I'll see you again
In the morning
When you rise again
And live another day
I know you're
Finally at home.

-Michelle Perkins-

Hope

Sunshine rushes in
Warming my face,
my blood
(my dreams)
Alight again after winter's emptiness
Like a forgotten womb
Alive with presence and possibilities
Choosing to go forward
Living in hope

-L. Wright-

While Drowning in Your Sorrows

While drowning in your sorrows, take a deep breath of hope. Out of the shouts of hatred, hold the hand of tolerance. In this life that drains you lifeless, rise up to help the helpless, and when love seems to have lost all of its power, then become a warrior and fight to give its name a more powerful meaning.

-Stacy Evans B.-

The Meadow

I lie here in the meadow
staring at the clouds
my mind, drifting
as time is ticking by
and as I lie there flowers grow
budding towards the sunlight
with dewdrops glistening
like diamonds in the grass
while birds are singing songs that soar
through the rustling of the leaves
and I for once, after so long
am finally at peace

-Lizzy in words-

Light Years Away

Thinking of you now, seems like 'm gazing
at my favourite star, it shines still, but I
know the light is from millions of years ago,
and the star might have ceased to exist long
back, but it is as real to me as the twinkle
in my eyes

- Vivek-

Unforgettable

Once the final prayer is done
and nothing more that can be said,
remember that I'm never truly gone,
I live on in your head....
You think back to our memories
and treasure what we had.
You can keep them safe in locks and keys,
the good times and the bad.
Although you may feel isolated,
no way to get around,
know this is a new path created,
for you to continue new ground.
It can make you feel terrified,
uncertain the future seems.
Who knows what adventure you will find,
but I will follow you with your dreams.
Just remember that I love you
and will you love for evermore,
because when you live, I live too,
in ways you didn't know before.
So, when you're feeling full of sorrow,
don't cry too much for me.
Share my wisdom like 'something borrowed',
and set our spirits free.

-Fay Collins-

Competition Winners

Broken Hearts : Healing Words, was born in a large part out of a writing competition held by A.B.Baird Publishing – these are the winners of that competition.

Grand Prize:

"What Will Remain" *Emily May Portillo*

First Runner Up:

"Pray For Us" *Greg Oman*

People's Choice:

"Light As A Feather" *Whiskey + Empathy*

Contributing Authors

To discover more incredible writing by the authors found in this anthology, please visit their writing pages on Instagram.

Abi Hayes	@abi_adventures_
Akshaya Premnath	@sweven____
Alick Bailey	@alickb1
Aliya Ameer	@aa_liy_aa1993
Alkesha Chaudhary	@alkeshachaudhari
Amy Littleford	@amylittleford.author
Angela Marie Niemiec	@angel_writer
Austie M. Baird	@glass_walls_life
Bianca van der Kamp	@vanderkampNL
Brianne Bowman	@brianne.bowman
Brianne Reilly	@whiskeygirlwrites
Carrie Fossier	@Word_Trove
Courtney Blackstone	@courtneyblackstone
Diya Nijawan	@musesofapoet
Eric Rolston [EDR]	@whenthesunrose
Emily May Portillo	@poetry.on.the.exhale
Emily Perkovich	@undermeyou
Fay Collins	@yaffiewritesstories
Gabriel Rodriguez	@thewordofgabriel
Greg Oman	@greg.oman
Greg Rowan Shearer	@grspoetry
Harshitha Satish	@mypenman.writer
J. Savarese	@borgo_savarese
Jamie Rhiannon Fehribach	@wildernessofpaper
Jason Morgan	@jasonscreationstore
Jereni-Sol	@jerenisolpoetry
Kathy Coutts	@kathleenflavia49
Krystal Centinello	@words2bfree
L. Wright	@cowgirllaw
Linda Lokhee	@lindalokheeauthor
Lizzy in words	@lizzyinwords

Mari Antoinette	@poetessofhearts
Mark Wayne	@MWSchutter
Michelle	@Michelles.poetry
Nikki C. Mercer	@Imagineexplorecreate
Odette Millar	@odi1a
Rachna	@rachna_writes
Reena Doss	@reenadossauthor
Samira Rahman	@samira.rahman666
Samman	@sammanwrites
Sinead McGugan	@sinead_mcguigan123
Stacy Evans Brown	@pearlsofpoetry210_
Starr	@Starr.poetry
Steve Zmijewski	@catchstevez
Vivek	@v_k_s__
Whiskey + Empathy	@whiskeyandempathy

Index

Made in the USA
Coppell, TX
09 December 2019